Morning Glories

Morning Glories

& Other Poems

Brooke Bognanni

RED HEN PRESS | LOS ANGELES, CALIFORNIA

Morning Glories

Cover and book design by Mark E. Cull

ISBN: 978-1-59709-389-7
Library of Congress Catalog Card Number: 2006938050

The City of Los Angeles Department of Cultural Affairs, Los Angeles County Arts Commission, California Arts Council and the National Endowment for the Arts partially support Red Hen Press.

Red Hen Press
www.redhen.org

First Edition

Acknowledgements

I would like to thank:

My beloved parents, Mario and Paula Bognanni, rich in heart, virtue, and love, whose sacrifices afforded me the best gift: education. With every word I write, I write their garden.

My mentors, whose lessons extend beyond the classroom, including: Stanley Johnson and Helen Underwood (much gratitude), Bill Hilgartner, Eileen Lane, Tad Jacks, Gayle Latshaw, Byron Forbush and the rest of Friends School who helped raise me. Ron Tanner, Karen Fish, Jody Bottum, Margaret Musgrove, John Jordan, Fr. Joe Rossi, Dan McGuiness, Charlie LoPresto, Brian Murray, Judy Dobler, Barb Mallonee, Ernest Liotti, Marty Kelly, Lia Purpura, and the rest of Loyola College who nurtured me. My producer Jo-Ann Rasmussen, Al Starr, Steve Tanner, my colleagues, and the rest of CCBC who fostered me. And the writers who have inspired me: Richard Wilbur, Robert Fulghum, Alice Walker, Maya Angelou, Ernest Hemingway, Dante Alighieri, Ronald Reagan, Flannery O'Connor, Natalie Standiford, Kai Jackson, and Suzanne Vega.

The great loves of my life, my friends and family who taught me that my most valuable lesson is the Truth: Cortney, Ashlee, Sfen & Whit, and especially Sydney and Beachy. The Miss America Scholarship Organization, Linda Stoltenberg, Michael Gormley, Christian Gullette, Marc Minkin, Jay Corckran, and Kim Tapper—one of the most valuable, extraordinary women I have known—and to the rest of my family, Dottie Feeley, Lucia Cedrone, and Mary Hedeman for believing in me. And especially my love and witness to my life, Jimmy Standiford—*it had to be you.*

Red Hen Press and Kate Gale, my remarkable editor and doppelganger, who was paramount to the birth of this collection, finding me on an opposite shore. My gratitude and appreciation is immeasurable. And also Mark Cull and Jennifer Smith.

My students, (especially Anthony, Maryl, Moe, Nick C. and Jamie) who have shown me that the only thing greater than inspiring young minds, is to be inspired by them, and who have encouraged this collection.

Table of Contents

III. *Growing*

IV. *Blossoms*

For my mother and father——every morning's glory.

I

Seeds

Open Hand

—For my mother and A. Walker

They are the hands of women
Who have braided bread
And their daughter's hair
The shape of the nail—
A January half-moon,
Reminding me of my own
Only with ridges that develop over time,
Like the wind-sculpted sands of a fleshy salmon desert.
Always the ridges;
Though faint in youth,
An age of dishes and gardens grain deep creases
While wearing away other stony monuments of this earth.
And in the rifts is a script for life;
We will learn from our mother's hands.
In their smooth roughness
Is the written message: "Sacrifice."
We learn to search for the story
As we looked for "Nina" in Hirschfeld's sketches.
Lines in her open palm tell a story—
A picture-book we never outgrow.
And on the other side
A milky-way of blue veins
Cuts through the spots
Which form now
Like the birth of stars
And are just as precious;
We will learn from our mother's hands.

The Hair

—For my father

Pulled from the morning drain,
Beached on the side of the yellowing
Porcelain tub:
A swirl of my father's hair
Like a poisoned centipede
Or pallid paisley printed on his brown tie
Hanging in the basement
Near a pile of things not discarded-
Enough to give away.
Curled into itself this evening
As a bleached seahorse, dry
And just as startling a discovery;
Why had I not noticed
The hair's slatey game?

auburn attempt

my mother had deep red hair
in old color-touched photos
from her teens in the 1940s—
a Judy Garland auburn
as if she herself were
meeting me in St. Louis.
in one, a voluptuous fifteen
holds her little brother,
thick waves scallop her high forehead—
her hair seemed almost breathing,
its own spirit rippling the world
of her face, freckled sandstorms, beautiful.

mine turned out darker, only hinting,
glinting of her's.
in a vain attempt of recapture,
like an unphotographed moment,
I turn now to the bottle—
a purple mystery liquid,
the same bottle I use on her
fine silkened silvers,
careful of the rattail comb
against the pinkening scalp
and try (as I must) to
cover her age as
mine is beginning to start—
if only my hair could be like hers then.
if only hers could, too.

Coloring

Mamma chides:
Child, color inside the lines.

Wonderwoman goes garnet red
Beyond the breast and crown—
The perfection of the woodpulp page,
A haloing blush, or
Silver and Sienna soldiers
Battling the barricade of line,
Pushing past the surface rock.
Cornflower, slender as the Ipanema girl,
Left too long to tan
On the piebald pink and white
Mother-crocheted shawl
Makes indigo ink,
A Rorschach marking
Tide could not wash away.
Next door, Miss Gloria has coffee with Cremora,
Candy red-tipped cigarettes, and free samples—
Avon's *Dusty Rose* enamel
On the skin that frames the little nail
Surfaces the lap of a pastel nighty;
Pointelle too soft to throw away.
Then at preschool, the project:
Ornament angel
Defiance angel
Separation anxiety angel—
Colored in
With black permanent
marker.

Innocence Lost Yields Grape Jelly

Aunt Betty came to teach my mother
How to can grape jelly in Ball jars
As I stood under our arbor and helped
Pick the purple orbs like bloody globes
A divinely proscribed prophecy
And felt the sting at seven
Behind the knee where the skin
Tenders the bird-like bone
And makes creases like lines in the
Trunk of a severed young tree
As the bee dropped among the heap
Of tendrils and leaves for the Greek
As I stood startled by the burning
Welt beginning to rise like a red balloon;
Later mother took me to the opening of
The new mall with a paste of baking soda
Weighting down the balloon and
Bought me a choco-vanilla swirl cone;
The next day over toast smeared purple
I told my father about the burning
And the yellow bee on its back

Her Unknown Daydream

My mother is lying across her made bed,
A queen on a king,
And a five-feet-two sponge
Sopping up the late spring breeze.
She should be ironing—
Sprinkling my father's shirts,
But the wedgewood linen curtains
Billow up like flags—
Perhaps sails of a ship beckoning
Her to surrender Sunday's chores
For daytime dreams.
She usually watches Lawrence
Welk on public television,
Hums along to Judy's clanging trolley,
Or pauses on Julia
Child cooking up Coq au Vin—
Pass the time
Press the yolk
Perhaps a light spray of starch
Clothe the wire hangars.
But today took a different tone;
Piles of clean laundry would have to wait,
Like my father;
In the quiet of the breeze,
The ca-caw of the blue jay children.
The metal plate of the iron, cool
Like her Sunday spring.

Record Player

In the basement today
Going through old boxes
In the wake of the sale
I stumbled across
My daughter's little white plastic
Mickey Mouse record player
And her favorite worn disc:
Casper the Friendly Ghost.
She would flip through the stiff pages
Of the accompanying storybook
Tea-stained and musty now
Until the scary part played
A sound something like the
Screaming monkeys of Oz
How she would freeze
In sweaty anticipation of these ghosts
Silently wishing I would call to her
But knowing I was preparing dinner
Her tiny voice brave and knotted
In vain attempt would whisper
"Mommy commear"
I wonder when she listened to these records
For the last time
Did she know she would forsake them
For different, newer discs
Did she know the sounds of the world
Were more frightening than Casper
As I stand here now
The next to hold her music box
And whisper
I'm here

Paula

The natural landscape of her hand
Freckled in piebald beauty
Nails ridged as scallop shells
Fingers furled-in, graceful

From blonde grasses
Comes the rhythm
Of snapping beans,
Green and dewy.
Overhead, the flapping
Wing of a bird—
That familiar blue heron—
Sounds in slow-motion

Like the desiring
Of her
Nervous beating
Heart
To freeze
Momentarily
Time

The Shoes

Cleaning out their apartment with my mother,
I am noble
Until I come across the shoes
Neatly paired at the base of his
Rusty, tweeded Lazy Boy
Smelling roughly of moth flakes and menthol—

My grandfather's small tan shoes, 8-wide,
He swiped with black polish.
His little shoes.
I am unnobled.

At the last viewing
I stood awkwardly behind my mother
Hearing her whisper
I'll be seeing you, Pop.

Years later, I stare at her rough, wide feet
Her silvery toenails like small dimes
And wonder what ever happened to
Pop's little shoes.

Violets Replanted

—For George Abbott

The azaleas are waking over my father
Who is kneeling in his uncle's garden,
The worn knees of his gray cargo pants
Moist and soil-stained like black gesso
Across a sky of charcoals—
Stained as his nails from pressing down earth
Into a pot of African Violets.
He is in his own imagery;
His eulogy still hanging like the surrender
Of a white laundered sheet
Freshly pulled from the water and
Pinned to the weathered line
With wooden clothes pins smooth as worry stones
From the oils of skin's constant rubbing.
The resemblance strikes me for the first time;
He is his uncle's starred flag
Clinging to the pole at half-staff
The way that generation clung to World War II.
He is his uncle's only son,
And his aunt widow-watches from the kitchen window
As the violets bleed across the soil now,
Purple Hearts for her green yard,
My father's replanting finished for this day.

II

Planters

Camille Monet and a Child in a Garden, 1875

Behind Camille, the flowers scream like poppies—
The result of his quick strokes of opaque bright red,
Warming behind this cool triangular woman who is mending
Her whites. Behind Camille,
The flowers, like buttons, are sewn into their background
Layer after layer of Green, Yellow, Pink gardening itself
Behind the auburn-haired Camille in lavender dress.
The child, unfolded from her, sits on the ground in her own lavender-blue.
The girl has a book, and a hair bow, and a tiny wooden horse.
Her little fleshy tones, in thin transparent paint,
Barely stain the gray priming. An observed moment or
Captured impression, poured.
Strokes of white, cerulean, woven with pink and black, render fabric—
The texture of Camille. Grass,
The same fabric only celadon and ochre, melts
From sharpness as he walks away from the easel,
Leaving Camille behind.

Poplars

—(*Monet*)

She stood there, cold, like a
Naked window—
Three or four strokes of cool colors
Dotted in the landscape.
Sharp vermilion notes make poppies—
His screaming little trademarks which
Flicker through the wildflowers of a
Broad meadow.
Grasses weed themselves among buds the
Color of fuzz from an unwashed peach.
In the distance, blue-pink haystacks
Birthed under seashell clouds
Swim in a sky as blue as
Gainsborough's Boy. And she just stood there,
A transitory woman with her back to the
Poplars. The wind in the grass swept
Past into the large trees,
Tickling the light to flash off the edges of
Fluttering high leaves.
The poplars, an entirely new vocabulary of
Brushstrokes, forced the simplest of
Landscapes—the commonest of fields.
But this impression awakens contemplation,
Startled, as the woman by the poppies.

Little Dancer

—For K.I.T.

She is Degas' graced muse
In wedding-blushed tulle:
Dance Rehearsal, 1874;
The impossible twist of Balanchine bone,
Arm curled back like the palest
Grosgrain ribbon.
The palette of a psychologist's daughter,
Sensitive as the change of a season—
Perhaps the green bending plie into spring.
He painted her in skirts
And satin shoes en pointe:
Dancer in her Dressing Room;
Sometimes in egg-blue chiffon
Tracing the knee like a child's finger;
Honey hair piled high as a nest or crown.
She is generous as this bountiful season,
In lilac flourish after the rains:
Three Dancers in an Exercise Room;
Skirt spreading across the canvas of the day
Like his delft-tipped fan brush.
She is painted in notes;
A white-wash C-major—
A birch-limb leg stretching on the barre.
City buildings blink their eyes
Against the glass panes of this studio,
And in a century or more,
Little has changed,
Except when he painted her then,
She wore a black velvet ribbon
Like the feathered throat of the lark.

The Irises

—(Van Gogh)

A backdrop of yellow,
Cheese yellow
Poupon yellow
Yellow as your weak skin,
Frames these Irises in a simple brush-
Stroke vase—
Also yellow,
Cheap engagement gold
Murky pond gold
An imitation gold leaf background.
Look at these sad Irises
Strokes of lapis, cerulean, indigo,
Violet, scarlet and white brushed together
Like your violent hair in the morning.
Dare the green serpent-tongue leaves
Stab through these Irises?
Random pineapple leaves or
Scissor blades slicing the dainty
Fleshy petals of the Irises.
The dying clump of lavender-blue
Brushes the table, sickly—
Bending at the waist like some
Proud conductor,
Some gardening old woman,
Some mourning child.
A withered clump,
Hyacinth-like, and drooping
Without an Easter fragrance.
If he smelled what he painted,
He painted them musty
Musty as this postcard and
Our musty love.

City Ride

The cows in the pasture blur into
Rows of corn which grow tall and become
Lights along the highway.
The lights in the tunnel are stroboscopic
Through the windows of the bus which
Become freeze-frame slides.
In one frame, she captures
A child standing against the
Backdrop of graffiti with
Corn-rows and fuchsia polka-dot shorts.
With eyes closing and pressing out
The light, she remembers the
Poet who died in Yeats' house, and
Wonders how deep the Suicides
Dwell in Dante's Inferno.
The sun is softening, reshading the
Bus in extreme chiaroscuro. Darkness
Falls drunken and heavy over
Cars and graveyards, pressing down
Upon houses and falling through
Windows—blanketing sleeping
Children who only know one kind of
Art.

Car Taps

The car graveyard at the end of the road
Lies casketed by aging gas pumps,
A line of marine soldiers
Hoses poised saluting
Battered machinery—
Ghosts mangled in the metal.
Windshields cracked, spattered.
After night class, I stop on the way home;
My fingers tighten around the pump.
Still, I listen to their requiem bells—
Steely tombstone songs.
Breaks squeal, the bow stops short on violin strings;
Bags bursting with air as white July fireworks.
Bodies of flesh beat like drums,
Their unnatural bass of bone and skin
Against plastic, rubber.
The horn sounds: a bagpipe moan.
Muffled symbols cry out their last wrath;
Wraiths of this night encircle their stones
Marking Celtic croons, African runes, Patriot's tunes.
My fingers release.
The nozzle drips dry.
I salute.
Drive off in this March night.

Augustine

It's the smell of things that burn
In their flammable ripeness
That catches my life-supporting nose
Through the car window.
Edges of these cornfields fray out
Of sight, driving by in late September—
The killing season for squirrels.
The fields fray and fray,
Quilting themselves into the patchwork
Of this land for yet another year.

This year I have watched
Color run from your hair
Like yesterday's sediments
Washed clean in an evening shower.
And July's showers, unrelentless as March,
Marched in bold and scared as a Vietnam soldier,
Tearing us all down
Tearing us in blinding gray
Green-gray
While the color still runs
And water pours over this late season
In avarice
Gray-green
Instead of catharsis;
It's too much for you—
The passing of the youth of the year
And in this taking,
I have my confessions, too.

Life Savers

Kelly. Real Blue-Collar girls. Kelly Girls.
 Temporary life-savers that come in fruity colors. Green.
  Kelly green. In Irish flags and preppie's pads
   that resound of bagpipes from Scotland with red-
    bearded ale drinking dancers. Gene.
     Gene Kelly. That retired tapper who sang in the
      Rain and danced in our sophisticated hearts. Queen.
      Grace Kelly. All of the beauty of a queen and the
       grace of her name who stole the hearts of sophisticated
        men from Monaco to Monte Carlo and who deserved much
        more royal highness than just a neat Princess. Keen.
        Keen Kelly. Kelly O'Brien. The Keenest, kindest kid
         I knew in elementary school. My Irish Kelly green-
          eyed friend from dance class who I used to play
           princesses with and pretend I was a secretary
            at school with . . . who moved away. Out of my life.
            Kelly O'. Kelly Oh. Kelly.

Di

Desiring the stolen moment
Of a life belonging not to one
And yet to every-one;
Enslaved by the bar-gilded flash
That ambiguous desire
The unequivocal seeing of the eyes
Of the morbidly curious.
Could any billionaire ever know
The cost of being loved too much?
In the swoosh of crepe, taffeta, ivory lace
In the twinkling of a starry crown—
The ever-present flashing click
Of a once welcomed weapon
Capturing, freezing forever the shyest of blue.
Sorried nations mourn.
And what is left behind:
Two young lads
Kilted plaids
A land not unlike our own—
A game of solitaire
With cards played out too early;
An ace of spades
Too quick to trump
The Queen of Hearts.

So-long, Mr. Green

It's a dance we'll all do;
Some fancy to the old soft shoe
While others rumble through with a rumba.
If we're lucky, we tango
In oranges and reds, satins and the rest.
But you, classic as Balanchine's muse,
Learned them all
And what we have learned from you—
Stepping through life
Through the rain
In song
Is as precious as
An American in Paris.
It's a dance I will remember;
In the rolling knolls
Of the Irish countryside
Where Gaelic banshees do a dance
That's hardly modern—
In the driving of my Kelly green car—
In the face of my own tango partner—
In the emerald ring on my finger—
You are in them all.
Spirit bright as lime lifesavers
Or light tapping patent leather
And graceful as the satin ribbon
Lacing up the leg,
Your final number—
A black-tie affair
A subtle slide in your sleep
A tap dance.
Taps.
So-long Mr. Kelly green
Gene.
We're dancing slowly
To the blues.

—In memory of Gene Kelly, d. Feb. 2, 1996

Struggle

Two men squabbled over an eight-ball or a striped red ball
And in the commotion someone scrambled
On to the felt-top pool table like
Jacqueline Kennedy sprawling over the trunk of the car.
The thin man with the Hitler mustache
Grabbed his inebriated comrade by the hair,
Tugging as if to straighten Mozart's wig,
And bent him to the bruised floor.
It could have been the paint-face girl
In the heels like "Prince" or Louis XIV
Who yelled "Jesus," or it could've been me;
I cannot remember.
But like a watcher who sees
Beyond the real or actual,
This struggle was as important to him
As Washington's wooden teeth—
I saw him there in the corner,
This friend I have known.
Though he saw me, he did not move away
From my glance or the fight
As if he could not
Hear or did not see—
As if he was not in this bar at all,
But somewhere else;
On a wall, framed or poised,
His legs fading into the smoke of their cigarettes
Like Michelangelo's brush resting in a glass—
The brush cracked, diffused, disappearing through the
Murky, clouded water of deluge that
Was this place.

With the Cart

In the twilight or a graveyard off 2nd Street,
The caretaker wheels a cart, collecting bottles.
He is a prisoner to the immense overgrown field.
Stones whisper names and dates worn away—
An age of sleet and wind.
Beyond the markers, and the two bushes,
And past the kneeling dandelions
There is a river—
Silver-gray as the gravedigger's hair.
And a memory of himself as that water—
An elongated sheen running, curling,
Seemed fleeting and distant.
He wondered what circumstance led to this—
Where the body of water lay casketed by the hillside—
Where the magnitude of darkness made black leaves.

The Quelling

Kelmer's pond,
Colored like graying wood pulp,
Is snoring beyond the heath.
A mallard is mourning there.
Yesterday her mate fell near the side,
A victim of some random shot.
Grubs have moved in upon him.
It took two hours for him to die.
A partial chain-link fence is
Kneeling near the water, seemingly
Out of place.
The duck sounds—
A knelling crosses Kelmer's pond;
She dives under.
Puffer weed explodes
Into this cool wind.

Winter Marsh

Thorton is down by the woodshed
Piddling, or doing what one does
In brown flannel.
His breath, like stuffing from a
Burst cat-o-nine tail,
Lingers and puffs in the air.
The startled yawning of naked
Birch branches mingled with
The barely audible sound of snow,
Tickling the rooftop of the cottage
Where Thorton's wife was decorating
an evergreen with real wax candles.
Thorton's failing eyesight caught
A glimpse of red—a cardinal,
Of child's mitten lost,
On a one-way path leading home
from school.
The snow—each layer swallowing
itself—poured over the glen
and the cottage
and the marsh,
disappearing into the white
of Thorton's hair.

Breaking a Record from 1922

The shock of cardinal
Punctuates the landscape of
White noise falling in slow motion;
His little carrot beak
Searches for Thorton's shelled peanut
Or a crumb for its bedding
Left by January's squirrels.
Tentative, he swoops in
Grounded inches from his find
While she looks on, brush-bound, in taupe.
His head points up, but bravery is only
A scarlet mask as he lifts,
Startled by the windy drift of white.
Surely he would've battled this snow in red armor,
But left scarcely a shadowed tint;
She followed in flight and silent disappointment.
Squirrel, in her fur coat camouflaging,
Flat as March on her belly
Her baby tail stubbed since birth
Went nut-praying.

Heron

Movement stills
Along the reedy bank
As a round onyx bead catches my gaze.
White-watercolor-blue pales,
Silhouettes itself against the mossy pines
And then begins again its feathery tai chi;
Movement in slow-motion
Like the wheaty spartina's salty reluctance
And then surrender in the wind.
Lifting a foot, definite, and placing it lower
On the bank with precision,
The neck curves to mimic human form—
The curve of a woman's arched back
The line of the neck to the shoulder
The stretch of early morning
As delicate as the oyster's pearl offering.
Movement slips
And disturbs the water's silken surface
The rippling of aqua shantung
Through a natural sanctuary
Like the sliver of silv'ry moon against evening.
Movement as reverence
Slender-bodied bird, silent as a moment
Into the preserve.

The Lake of Swan's Departure

The white swan pulsated
And lingered across the lake;
Wings emanated, her spirit broke
from the boundaries of that place
which reflected always that first
hopeful celestial twilight.
Watching from a distance
Her eyes streaked across the sky, darkly.
And lowing near the water,
a salmon-colored sun
which the bird could never reach
even in emphatic flight.
In her absence,
the bottle remained,
wedged between some sedimentary rock.
The sea bled the thick, corked glass
Into that water—
The lake of swan's departure.
And if in some exquisite wake,
the bottle is broken,
shattered pieces will disperse themselves
into flowing seas or brooks,
fragments swallowed by Bishop's fish;
bloodied gills staining the surface,
grabbed by the dark-eyed swan
Before bursting
Into unknown flight.

The Rising

—9.11.01

cinder
like some
Holo-caustic dream
falling
powdering
an infant
duck-white
in unexpected
dusk

The Purse

The yellow wicker
Island purse
Is trimmed in
Brown leather—
A native's pathway
Whose toes are
Ashen with
Toast-colored
Earth.

A Tearing Down

Last year's possum is in the shed,
Albino, with silver-glow eyes.
He comes out for dusky ritual
Moving across the back lawn,
Foxlike as if to use a diving rod,
Toward the grape arbor.
Once he curled himself around
The vines for an intoxicating
Midnight snack, but tonight
His discovery was fruitless,
The webbed arch torn down;
Nothing remains of the leaves,
The tendrils, the wine-ready fruit.
What is left, a gray and
Rusting frame, is stark and
Barren, still waiting for him—
One end snapped in a
Constant wind.

III

Growing

An Auspicious 4th

A noise, a whistle, popping corn,
The dropping of some bomb
The beating of my heart
Begins this illusion of
Challenger in flight
Or a blue electric jellyfish pushing through the harbor,
Streaking tentacles lingering.
Imagine Eve's tempter squirming, sperming,
In a black gesso sky.
One, a pink blooming flower captured
Through time-lapse photography,
Another, a green spotted mushroom top.
Are we under the dark blue sea,
Seeing reefs of living red coral?
A single raindrop magnified,
Breaking and e x p l o d i n g
As it hits a glass sky.
Show every miniature purpley nebulous milky way
Each spark independent of the other,
But congruently forming a whole
Galaxy—perfect and round;
A form dictated only by the
Burning dissipation of the white spark.
Every golden shooting star in the universe
Is coming together in the sky that is overhead—
Leaving behind a foggy, smoke-filled air,
That gives night an alien-green illusion
Of very early dawn.

Marigot Beach

The morning after Thanksgiving
The ocean came lapping at my picture window.
Restless through the night
She mimicked my heart beating weary,
But unable to slow worry.
I could not help but go to her
In comfort, for comfort
Plopping myself, in black shorts, in her lap.
I will stay until you come,
I whispered, while I waited—
Coaxing her like an infant trying
To take her first step.
I whispered until finally the foam
Met my peanut toes like a first frost
And I could make peace with this place.
Pausing for a moment in fog-misted
Sand, I looked forward
Counting four layers of folding algae seas,
Recognizing the sound of goodbye.
For, it is high tide
and
This is how I pray.

Everyone Is Escaping Something

I was as out-of-place there
As the baby grand that sat in the middle
Of this country cabin bathing
Honey-colored in the morning sunlight.
The same sun tickled the valley and the
Clear water and the pale blue berries of the
Elderberry bushes pushing their way along
The side of the log house.
The old woman told me about living off the grid—
About making wine and pancakes with the
Crunchy, bittersweet elderberry—
About the beatitude that flows from virtue.
In the afternoon, I heard the metal blade of a
Crosscut saw going through the trunk of a cedar,
Making a bright song that filled the people here in Gloria.
I noticed the dove's tweet from a barbed-wire fence,
So unlike the crying of the saw.
It must have gotten late as I curled in the hammock
Under a summer-white sheet, because the
Locusts were drawing near and the trees made
William Blake-like silhouettes against a darkening sky.
I knew the people here were sinewy people,
And I knew this land was about tolerance and distance,
About temperance and prudence,
But I did not know why I had come
Or how, faithlessly, I would ever, ever find my way back.

Folds

—For S. Vega

She sat on the bench
Sprawling something on a piece of loose-leaf
About Calypso or a Gypsy.
The trees were losing leaves,
Shedding bark like a snake sheds skin.
A pause.
A red grapefruit
Peeled, sectioned.
And using her thumbnail she shucked the zest
From under the others and turned again
To the paper—
White, organized, and margined.
She waited for a moment.
Picking up the sheet, she let her ideas
Fold and overlap—
Having origamied into some shape,
And looking down into the palm of her
Open hand sat a revelation—
A loose-leaf crane.

Lilac Time

The students in the quad are lilac-drunk
In this late-April hush before summer.
Voices slur behind the breeze
Ripe with orchid fragrance,
Yawning like winter,
Cordoned by these bushes—
These flowers that stay only briefly,
Like a guest for Sunday brunch at the house.
They are the artist's momentary impressions
Captured on a leafy canvas—
Blossoms opening as the sun sets;
How the sky is colored just for them
In celebration of their fleeting beauty.
They are situations; temporary
Even if we do not want them to be
The way watery laughter subsides.
Their edges begin to burn brown by mid-May—
The fragrance fades,
Colors blending into the drying earth
Leaving something missing behind
Forgetting their carousing ways
Drying out
Forgetting what they brought—
A hostess gift cupboarded away,
The quad quieted in the stillness of summer.

Loyal

Fingering lightly the spines
Of the familiar books standing in attention
On the built-ins of my mentor's office,
I am here now, borrowing her inspiration
As she sabbaticals herself
Into pages awaiting their birth.
The pinking two-o'clock sun
Reveals dust, particles suspended
Like a burst puffer weed
Wished upon by summer's child.
Unaware, I find myself sitting
Entranced by a lowing shelf
Of Norton's *Nature Writing*,
Audubon, and *Bay Country*.

Outside the windows to the courtyard below,
Benches wait for me as they used to do not so long ago.
On one, a tweed in silk bowtie pipe-smokes loyalty.
Graying priests pass youth in the quadrangle
Where conversations hush like Hemingway's "White Elephants."
Piano, like water music, drips from an open thresh
Onto evergreens standing like graduates.

In the evening, on the path to Jenkins Hall,
I wonder why the Ides of March
Always make my eyes water,
Why spring is strong enough to force winter's retreat,
Why the chalk graining my fingerprints
Has left my hands, like my mother's piebald hands,
Arid and crackling red
As a throat cleared during lectures
On Dante, Freud, Wilbur, and epiphanies.

I am here now, in the turret
On the way back to her office,
My office—
A Peaceable Kingdom,
Watching from the top
The catharsis—
The snowflakes
Like angels
To welcome me
Home.

Mentor

—For J. T. Bottom

Handsome Philosopher
sitting on his bench
drinking coffee
outside of the pristine college
reading the Confessions
of St. Augustine.
Afraid of death and dying—
afraid of not educating the children
at home.
Handsome Philosopher
people watching,
smoking Merit Ultra Lights.
Shaking hand
flips back hair and
turns the page.
"Beyond the pen, the paper,
must be a passion in the language."
Self qua self and
Being is being being.
And what you've taught me
you will never know
because you're so afraid of dying.
You in your British tweed coat
with cuffed trousers
and a twister for a
wedding band—
You starling
You ordinary Jesus.

Simple Gifts: Friends School

Beyond the twelve-paned office window
Where a spider is caught between the frames,
Yellow-pink light of early morning
Brushes awake the August-green foliage.
Silent rustles catch the daydreams
Of the person next to the glass.
She thinks of her life in equation;
Part is hopeful fantasy.
But hope is too much: *wish*.
The computer sleeps still on the desk,
And the phone has failed to wonder.
And in this Quaker silence,
A reverence for this place:
Palma Non Sine Pulvre.
It is different now, in its demystification,
And this worker has graduated from here before.
There is a longing from the leaves
Green with an eager ambition,
For it is August and
An orange-brown September
Burns near the Meeting House,
Where soon children, scarlet and gray,
Will wake this sleepy place.

Sewing Night for Young Writers

A quilt
A fabric
Not for Frost's winter
Not for AIDS
Not their great-grandmothers'
Time-weathered heirloom.
A quilt
Stitched by my Night Children
Who follow the babbling brook's edge
In search of sustenance
Picking up along the bank
Raw red silk shantung
For a red-headed tapestry
Or lily-of-the-valley linen for the bride
Who'd rather elope.
The terrestrial textile of a nurse-mother—
An Ackerman in her own right
With story unfolding;
Or one who sings shades of a Greek-blue history
With eyes that belong to generations of her women.
Two dark-haired lovers waltz the blade, the edge of shore,
The pebbles slip beneath their camouflaged feet
As another who travels emerald countrysides
Searches for the pleasure of pubs, plaids,
A swatch of black-watch to add.
Searching supernaturally, finding his own way,
One is the snapping of a twig, a button dropped,
Following the scent of decay—
Of things once breathing, but stumbles instead
Across the blond one who sits lost in the electric fur of moss,
Feet inches above azure water,
Dreaming of the greening fabric of rip-tide.
There is the one who drew the coming-of-age,
One of Bly's boys beating the fire to collect childhood's cloth.
Then the spinner: working the loom

In a hooded rhythm around which others lurk longingly—
An actor closing the casket lid, assigning color, too much for this room.
My Night Children:
Their quilt spreads along this brook;
A community of writers making their own way.

The Teacher

—For Helen Underwood

You are James Joyce
Consciousness streaming
Or Virginia in a room of your own
With yellow wallpaper

You are James Baldwin
Bringing Harlem to our hands
Telling it on the mountain
And singing the blues

You are Mother Teresa
Scraping Calcutta
After the streets flood with rain
On a waning sienna afternoon

You are Toni Morrison, beloved,
Quilting the children into their roots
Dancing in bare feet
Ashen purple in the dust

You are Flannery O'Connor
Stirring short-stories and mock turtle soup
Southern spittin' bubblin' simmerin' your jive
In teal peacock feathers like a fly's eye

You are a crimson apple growing
About to split open
Dropping rolling stopping breaking under-wood
The seeds like children, dispersed, green growing.

Silverware

The clamor for the drumstick
at the children's table
of those anxious to circumnavigate
saying Grace
diminishes under Wedgwood clinks
from wine-touched relatives
The middle boy seems to be entranced
By a wire hanger mobile.
On the thresh of the front door;
An unbeknownst science project from long ago
where the flattened fork balances harmoniously
with a bent spoon and tarnished knife.
He had not been looked at,
but looked over
As the sounds from the dining room
Became muzac for the performance
of the mobile's drafty dance.
How crestfallen he was to learn,
Not of the feast finished in his absence,
or missing Grace
(though he was as filled as Tuesday's Child),
but of the mobile's finish:
Honorable Mention.

Proper USAge

The nebula opens in space, unseen, your heart
utters its great beats in solitude. A new era is
coming in. Gauche as we are, it seems we have
to play our part.

—Adrienne Rich

The florist is late in delivering a dozen white daisies,
And why they're important, who really knows—
Except that this room could use some brightening.
In this basement, there's a boredom to the business
That assembles this room.
There's the smell of chartreuse vinyl office chairs
Undermining the lemon airwick on the desks.
So I imagine these desks as sleeping elephants
Along a dusty bank sloping into cool muddy pools.
There are only two phones and they never ring
Because we do not give them a chance;
There's never a free line here.
So I take another computerized sheet from
Under the glass pinwheel paperweight
And practice silently the next name.
Even the phone has an odor, and I imagine
A shower pouring from the holes of the receiver in
Eucharistic cleansing on this failing day.
After I close up here, I will volunteer myself
To the house and the husband and the striped apron.
The chicken needs stuffing with thyme.
Time is running out for some campaign.
Tonight I will fill the glasses with champagne—
Gold like the center of this single daisy
Stolen from a late delivery;
Gold like a stellar apparition, twinkling
And disappearing from a fixed eye.

Prosecution

In the dream, the judge
Played that game with me;
Persecuting the prosecutor
For bewitching one accused—
But spending my life on the
Assignment of blame
I knew I was no
Adulteress of jurisprudence.
The defendant's lie opened
Just enough to slip in
A white silken sash—
A blindfold A surrender
A gag A weapon
Wrapped around the
Neck of the betrayer.
And the one who betrays
Is black-cloaked,
Calling with a meal
And red wine,
Offering last rites,
Rites of passage,
A righteous penalty—
While I spend my
Days taking away
Death's authority.

Roadside Homage

Memorials for ordinary days
Roadside cones with flowers of cornflower blue that say
DAD
Or towering electrical poles that scream
Into the sky and root their way into the earth
With plastic pink carnations necklacing the base.
Alongside highways, winding woodsy streets, and well-worn avenues
Ubiquitous pauses with hushed significance
Rest unburnished in sorrowful heaps
More frequented than unrequited love
By those unaware as usual;
They are commonplace to strangers
Who never seem to notice
Or pretend not to;
Someone's next-door neighbor with morning glory blue eyes
Who failed to negotiate an S-turn while coming home too late from the fair
Births a sudden garden by the valley road from his mother's last visit
Careful not to disturb the landscape
As an automobile once did.
That which is left behind
Grows
If only to linger on
Until the next rain
Or the next.

The Beach

—For Elizabeth Bishop

The red sun bulges in the six o'clock sky,
Staining the sand with salmon blood.
Summer yawns.
Its head nods
As on-lookers stand with coffee on the pier.
Cheesy "Ocean Gallery" landscape paintings feed
Boardwalks and artists
Who try to capture images in acrylic.
The sun—
A red balloon
Or boxing glove—
Reflects radiance on coconut oiled flesh.
A conch is captured by a native
Who braves the algae-green waves.
Some creature fights and splashes in the shell.
Scattered like peanuts
Are the shells of horseshoe crabs
Who could not whether the tropical depression.
How the sun is straining
Like the thirteenth labor of Hercules
Burning
Burning out of sight
Snatching the last hour of heat as
September burnt skins retreat from the shore.

Persied's Peak Showers

August's meteors surround this little
    gray-and-white house
A stone's skip from the beach
    on High Sheriff Trail,
Although it is too dark to see
    even the sky.
I imagine the face staring back at me
    in the glass wants in,
Out of the blank blackness that carries
    away clarity and form
Like some mad painter's failed
    experiment in chiaroscuro.
In the light of my mind's eye I see the pines
    tumbling toward bleak heavens
But through this glass, darkness with
    her potent invisibility ticks away.
And though I see, tonight I am in blind-search
    for end-summer's shooting stars;
So many stars, like Wordsworth's insects
    in battle to show themselves or
Clothe the dusk in a whiter gown
    for some constellation bride.
Where instead darkness rains
    down on this roof like a curse;
Too dark to see the sky, I pretend,
    pretend at being alive.

Checkout Girl on Tuesdays

The red-aproned checkout girl at Safeway
wears a grimly smiling scar around her neck;
Its edges have soften liked a chiffon scarf,
though I notice it every Tuesday beyond muffins
and milk, produce and pudding.
It glistens like a 10-karat gold choker under her chin,
framed by her gold-plated hair fraying at the hem.
The slice hints the mandarin-pink of an unfresh wound,
though still, she rarely meets eyes with her customers.
My eyes seem to make the mark extend as a
rubber-band reaching from right year to nearly left,
so I lower my gaze to search for exact change
as if the whole of it might make her job easier,
and hand her over the thirty-two cents,
noticing from brow to nose, to petal-pursed lips
the question mark in her narrow face.
Whose blade made this delicate chain,
permanent as a tattoo, a reminder of a tearing in time?
What modernist etched this bending line—
edging the throat like a clover-leaf taken too fast
across the beltway of her skin?
Had he tried to sand the plane of her neck
To smooth his own jagged edge?

Your Bad Idea

They place you with your brothers.
They fold you and transport you with
The others who are joined to you by thread.
They told you it was
A bad idea.
They watched your skin become a sickly calico,
And watched the snow coating the ground like
The crumbled aspirin that coated your tongue.
They knew it had been
A bad idea.
They pulled back the white brocade curtains,
The ones that hide the windows in your room—
The ones that have yellowed with age.
They stood in your doorway
And watched you looking toward the light,
The light that seeps through the place where
The curtains meet.
The light was so yellow it was almost pink.
They watched the product of
A bad idea.
The pan on the floor held garnets
Or maybe crystallized blood.
They spoke to you,
The ethereal gypsy, with the needle-marked arm,
And watched your black hair streak like a zebra's.
They said you were murrained when
The aids came to take you home.
They all knew about
A bad idea.
They sprinkled your gray ashes over
The dead sea
And started your quilt.
They named your panel
A Bad Idea.
They made it red so
All would see when

They placed you side to side with your brothers.
Now everyone would know about
Your Bad Idea.

Summer Job

Why does this opening interest you?
asked the charcoal-suited man
with a charcoal handlebar mustache,
as if about to burst out in a barbershop tune.

I've been doing some research on grief counseling,
and you know my godparents.
I did not tell him
I heard the money was good.

You'll need a dark blazer,
and always wear stockings and a skirt,
even if it's 90 degrees.
Expose little.

On the floor, I brought Dixie cups
of fountain water to a widow,
emptied black metal pails filled
with rolled white tissue,
or vacuumed uniform tracks in the rooms.

Sometimes I stood at one end of the long hall,
carpeted like the Yellow-Brick Road,
breathing in thick tiger lily,
hearing muffled sighs at the other end
like an Auden elegy,
and wondering how much longer
until I could dim the lights.

Once I took a phone message for Andy,
who was in the basement prep room
when the intercom was out.
Grasping dark chiffon in one hand,
I descended the slippery yellow stairs
and tapped open the door.

I remember her clearly,
like the mannequins
my grandmother took me to see as a child
in Macy's department store window.
She sat upright, naked on a silver gurney;
her arm stiffly extended toward me,
fingers contorted as if tied in some unfamiliar bow—
her brittle hair in rusty curls
framed an aged-plastic face.

My mouth opened as if to scream,
like rounding the corner
in the fun house on the pier,
but no sound came forth, no breath.
I handed over the message
as Andy droned about the difficulty of dating
in his line of work—
death's a turn-off, he said.
And I returned to Dixie cup duty.

At the end of the night,
the widow gave me a basketed philodendron.
Years later, I lay in bed watching the clock
flip to 12:34, my favorite time.
The theater of my eye grows dark,
And I still see her image—
Plastic, naked, extended.
And think of the price paid for summer work.

Wretched

When you can feel the rotation of the Earth,
Like the motion of an endless carousel
Where the barker is supernaturally loud,
Urging the grimacing ponies forward
Spurring them to blur you to green—
And you pull back their flowery reins
In vain attempt to stop their exploiting,
And hear only the flush that spirals down
What has been inside and
Once was good like milk and honey;
When you plead for relief
From circle to circle only to find
Inferno cold at the bottom;
When tickets are sold for over four hours
To this ride that waves in and
Subsides in philosophical intensity,
Testing the passenger's endurance
In some hellish, twisted Olympics—
And even the softest feminine whisper
Uttered in the supple yellowish-pink light of
Morning is suddenly evil as a cackling spectral clown;
When a glimpse in the mirror of a hue unbecoming,
Follows the hollow echo of knees on tile
In search of mercy
And the taste that builds is of neither milk nor honey,
But forces the ride to dead-end into a bed with
Posts like an angel's wings;
When you linger there
Waiting out Satan's State Fair
You know he has revealed himself
As Migraine.

Vertical

—For Jamie

Startled
By the early
Morning sight
The tangerine
Goldfish
Vertical
In the bowl
Centering the
Kitchen table
Vertical
Like a teabag
Extended from
A stained string
Caught still
On that invisible hook
Vertical
Unlike the passing
Of days
Whose decisiveness
Does not wait for
Me to understand.

IV

Blossoms

Morning Glories

— For Sydney

I could have sworn I saw
Morning glories crawling through the snow
Twining themselves up the barren
Metal frame of the grape arbor.
But I must have been dreaming the earliest of dreams.
Flowers as blue as bird feathers, and even
Yellow and a little green were growing despite
The day that awoke into a 60-degree fog,
Cleared to a hurricane rain
Dried to near tornado winds
And chilled the air to 15° F
Expelling showers of snow
And sleet and, as a magic spell,
Wickeding the streets to black ice.
So the earth is expelling your sickness
As I sing to you: *Grace will lead you home.*
I have struggled to remember how it begins,
Though I recall *"But deliver us from evil"*
And whisper this to your quivering chest.
I am torn;
Sufferance has puffed and ruffled you,
But I am not ready to say good-bye.
Standing, vigilant, I watch as you seem to slip away
In weakness as the newborn foal's legs
Struggle to stand for the first time in birth
Only now I am watching you go.
With closing eyes you sense my tears and are
Lulled by my voice softly humming, helpless.
This evening you have puffed yourself
    closed
Like the sleeping of a yellow-blue morning
    glory
Or the shamrock plant whose leaves close
 into themselves like praying hands.

33 Degrees

The impotent wind has failed
To sweep upward
The bending reed,
Solitary in a blonding field,
As Hermes might have done
Successfully, toward
A quenching azure-blue sky
And drenching salmon sun.

I am there—
Where every unrequited
Song ever written
Is accommodated
In the landscape
Of your eye.

And every reedy streak
In your autumn hair
Tears into me
As the first drops of rain
Verging at 33 degrees
Acid themselves into
My blushing, rushing cheek.

You are there—
Beyond pebbled pathways
And trails thick-green
With foliage
Where thoughts are bred
To cross your mind
But never be considered.

Maybe in a time before
When skirts swept low and slow
And glances meant at least as much
And hearts verged on 33 degrees
We were there together
In that breathing,
Luck-green field

Instead of lonely
In the golden-white grasses
Bent
And living with chronic pain.

Encounter

A woman whose hair
Was not quite red
But beyond brown
Crossed the street.
She was going
To his office
Where he sat behind
A desk suited
In navy wool
Happy but not
Surprised to see her.
She knew why
He removed his glasses,
As she had done before,
And this transparence
Reminded them both of an
August diner which
Couldn't be more
About May and December.
How careful he was
Hugging her in front
Of the doorway ajar;
And how short their time;
And how carefully he
Used the word,
"Woman."

Brandy and Wood

—For M.K.

Autumn's familiar dappled light
Shows itself in golden vanilla
Across the wooden bench
Where I sit again wondering
If *thirty* could ever need *twenty,*
In view of his corner office—
The Tudor building where windows
Permit a glimpse of the suited figure
Behind a rosewood desk
Leaning back in his burgundy leather chair.

If I was brandy
I would be old
But to him I must seem summer-young
Shrouded in lilac innocence;
Only I know the secret strands of silver
Etching their way through my auburn hair.

But years are spent growing a tree
Hearty enough for the stuff of desks—
Those traditional desks
In collegial offices,
Or tables gracing the formal dining rooms
Of those involved in some domestic circumstance
Where newspapers are read
On lazy weekend mornings
And red wine, or perhaps brandy,
Is sipped in evening's goblets.

His wood wears a silvery coat
Protecting a cherry-stained surface
From liquored trickles
As couples sit across from each other;
Maybe light, in waves, reveals a scuff
Or the indefatigable silence between them.

M.G. — 1

And I know now the answer
To that question which has hidden itself,
Dormant some nine years;
That very query which
When asked in his
Familiar pensivity
Sat there unanswered
As a little red-headed child
Pushing funereal questions

So rumors whisper his name
A name dormant
While others tried impotently
To teach me
More than him;
A vocabulary
Among other things
I absorbed with bewilderment at 15
Pensive was his favorite word—
A somewhat disconcerting dark-green word

So many times I have tried and failed
To replace his world with a brighter green
The shade I have come to know—
Perhaps verdant, kelly, evergreen
Green persimmons—
An eloquentia perfecta
But California's gold
None less the fool
Has found his way back to this shore
And I will drive off in my emerald ship
In search of Lovegrove Street and
Maybe a glimpse of him grown—
The man he always was in naïve image

And I know now the answer
To the question:
What is beauty?
In the center of an apple
The sweet succulence of a gala apple
Beyond the core
There is a hollow;
The epiphany of the fruit
Revealing a flower
Yellow-pink within
Imagine nature's negative space
Petaling itself within that autumnal flesh
When only a mouth can uncover the secret
The knife never revealed

Why had it taken nine years
To answer such a question
To know such a truth
Such contemplative beauty—
And to find him again?
If only I could find him again
To place in his left hand
An apple.

༚

M.G. — 2

More an alley
Than a street
I understand
Running into
Downtown
Baltimore
An evocation
Of a city

I am running
On my own path
From home
White Nikes
Keeping pace
Through the
Blinding golden
Piebald light
Of autumn

Fall's forgiveness
Breathes deep
In my chest
Like a waking
Hibiscus
As some barking
Dog spurs
Spirits of swiftness

Though the burning
In my legs vines itself higher
Challenging the creeping chill
I hardly feel the contact with the
Pavement underneath
As my mind

Along for the jog
Rides separate
Floating above
Remembering departures
Some nine years ago
Adding to California's gold

But to find him again
Back after so many years,
How so much has changed with autumn
Save the heart
Whose memory like a majestic elephant
Is still running triumphant
Beyond the brook
Reflecting a lowing salmon sky

Maybe I will take a drive
I will drive and drive
And bite down on the irony
Finding him again
After so many years
Living on
Of all places
Lovegrove Street

M.G. — 3

Finding his way
Back home
Finding California's gold
In Baltimore
I wonder if he found
The Way

Remembering how
His ailing grandfather
Brought him finally
Faithlessly at eighteen
To his knees kneeling not
In Hope
But in Shadow
As the story started

The priest
A betrayal
Friend unfound
From Caritas
To heart of stone
Forgetting the way to
His House
Unquestioning questions

Now in more years
Than there are angels
He is home
But does he remember the
Stained glass
The coffee-stained earth
Covering his grandfather
The sustained Hope
I tried to bunch in his hand
Like a white linen hanky?
I wonder if he found the way
My Irish Dante

Gypsy

My love for you rivers as deep as the veins in
Green marble and is as defined as the

Lines in my palm. Your memory needs protecting
Like a surgeon's hands. Your rarity, black

Sand, absorbs colour manifold and turns
Into one. Your flight, like Leda's Swan, reminds me

Of how I felt the year my smiling pumpkin was
Stolen, and since, my thoughts have been the

Clarity of seedy jack-o-lantern mush. Tweeded
Gypsy, your sculptor's hands will shape another—

But I can still see those English teacher-eyes,
Leaving me here, winged, waiting to be born,

Under a bruise-blue sky—thunder is coming
From the west, distant, but moving closer.

Parson's Island at Fifteen

Gray and rust and reedy,
we walked the perimeter in maybe two hours.
The early March-barren land revealed broken,
naked tree limbs—
Perfect walking sticks.
The pheasant took flight as we neared, streaking the sky
with feathers the color of the impressionable clay underfoot.
One unsured side of the cliff
emptied unexpectedly into the bay
as if the cliff itself was stopping
a minute to watch the setting sun—
The sun was so pink it was almost salmon.
Someone jumped off an edge
lowing to a small pebble beach,
confirming the water's chill,
squatting to thumb a shell propped against
some seaweed in the shallow of the water's gulping.
Later, in the panorama-room of McCormick House,
I watched the tiny boats and water foul,
while others backgammoned.
I remember the earthy greens of the felt-top billiard table
and of the empty bottle we encircled.
But I could not forget him;
His absence would not let me—
And despite my cold, I could smell the musty,
Sea-salt air lingering in the room of this big house
on this tiny island
in my hair and on my school sweatshirt
and in my pillow,
though I did not sleep at all
that night on Parson's Island.

To Know

False prophets,
Those eyes of morning-glory blue
Because they do not belong
To a student of the morning.
Blooming fully after dark
As a crimson-caped creature,
A creative mind reveals itself
And sheds its skin
Of banker's navy pinstripes.
And what emerges is a memory
Greening every elephant
In Tanzania—
Resuscitating what Medusa
Had long turned granite-gray.
Take my hand;
Be the first and last
And swim with me to the
Islands of Memory.
We will walk the orchid shore and
You can collect your bombshell
With glints of red running wild through her hair.
Linger on the dunes beyond those reeds
And we will sing late like gypsies
And be richer and darker than
False prophets.

Water's Grace

Atlantis, precious as the
Vanilla Orchid whose fragrance
Makes a tromboning lure—
Jeweled, perhaps a ruby pyramid
Whose pointed ends like a compass
Uncover the under-azure
Red Roads of Bimini,
Vining their way across the globe of the eye
As paths of mystery
Clouded, silty, in pipe smoke
Lead to a jaded sea dragon
Behind an impossible tomb,
Or an epiphany inside of a golden apple,
Borne like a secret waiting to be told.
Water, a Shroud of Turin
Sheeting her king—
domed in briny preserve;
A mummy in seaweeded wrap
Clasping left-handed the map to
Childhood's ship, lost at sea's floor,
Submerged beyond latitude and longitude,
Defying the atlas looking-glass.
Look closer still at those lady-like Red Roads,
Arrows to the deepest oceanic blue
Even Columbus could never uncover
The ghostly treasure, a priceless penny,
Water keeps:
Atlantis, *lost you know.*
Found. *At last.*

Iridescent

—For D. Calloway

In late August
Along the coast
He spotted a conch
Brought in by the undertow
While counting porpoises
Beyond the frothing surf.
He rescued the pink
And white swirling mass
Risking his pants and sneakers
Before the shell was carried, unseen.
So iridescent and beautiful,
Polished by the rolling sandy brine—
The ocean's own musical composition
He held now in his smooth palm,
A spiral staircase to what is held inside.
A cyclone spinning still,
Gathering strength as it nears land
Landing like a mourning dove
Perched in his hand;
He held her to his ear
And though he could not see to the heart
He heard the whisper—
The secret mourning song—
The conch's only tell.

The Surface

—For Anthony

Surface of regret
A yellow-bellied fear
Warbling a
Sharply smooth spoken word
Where all is inside-out,
A black cotton, washed:
It looks worse than it is...

Surface of rhythm
A coupling of Paolo and Francesca
Still trapped in an inner Ring
A syncopation
Of green wheels on the same track;
To share, inevitable.

Surface texture
Tense as bloody silk
A first impression
Of the Wordsmith
With features superceding the superficial.

The surprise of the water's surface
As the body rises through the blue
Towards the face of a solid—
Southern wisdom, ageless.

Surface of sorrow
Cool like pewter
Orchid as knowledge's sky
Bound in ink and canvas
Ever-still arm's length away.

The Paper Cut

Closing his book on the night's chapter
I ran my lips across the edge
Where the pages come together in
A gray silken grosgrain ribbon
Much like the satin border of
My childhood blanket rubbed smooth and
Cool as wind-swept November sand.
Passing under my nose like a rite,
The pages smelled of sawdust
Or blood drying in the nail bed
Of nurses in Da Nang,
And I imagined him jungled
As if born to that time,
And was thankful for his unvisited
Wall that would never bear *Calloway*.
But these fragments are displaced
Like my bird body in the water of his mouth—
Light as his six-word inscription
Penned in secret on an early page—
Though discovery forbids the one he wanted to write
When he tucked an American Flag
Like a bookmark in the crease of sixty-five
Where words like
Carnivale   masked   mouth   seawater
Sailed the paper surface plane like gondolas.
In the sudden tasting of what I smelled,
I ran my tongue along the dune of the lip
Discovering I had gone against the blade of the page,
A Lady Macbeth for the millennium,
Parting the skin more oceanically than expected,
Though I have always heard
Mouths heal fast
Fast as azure August
Fast as his summery book.

The Last First Weekend in June

I am in a breathing photograph
One I have seen before
Where blue light seems solid,
Its smooth surface hurting my eyes
As sun pours its raw ostrich yolk
Over this captured day,
And the ground-even pool
Blends like sky's slope to earth.
Jay is by the grill, twisting his slick bacon fingers
In a spice-stained linen apron imprinted
With the fading word, "McCormick,"
Cheek-kissing drowsy girls 'good-morning' as they pass
Bound for the main house where orange juice or
Black coffee has been waiting patiently near a
Bowl of over-ripe, untouched gala apples.
This time I stay by the lonely, still pool
Thinking as I sit in a white-and-green chaise, fuchsia
Million Bells waking to their own ringing fragrance,
That this must be my last trip here,
Transforming my eyes, now lenses of a Nikon
Transfixed on this blue heron perched beyond
The gaggle of swans just off land.
He is silver, almost dusky, and knows I watch,
For he is feather-quiet, motionless,
His black marble eye cold against my gaze;
He knows I won't be coming back
As I close my eyes against the light
And hear the shutter release.

The Decision

Red potted geraniums skirted the pool,
Sticking straight up into the wind
Commanding respect,
Pinking buds fighting against their nemesis
That must've kicked up after 4:30 this morning.
By noon, the umbrella, forest-thick,
Surrendered, splintered, and
Bay disguised herself as ocean,
And we make decisions that cannot bend
Geraniums the other way;
They fold—
Theses choices that cannot be undone,
Defying Serenity;
Unlike the red heads of the flowers,
They were neither Courageous, nor Wise.
There's no changing the way the wind blows,
And it has passed through—
The extent of the damage, yet to be discovered.

The Affair

The decision to go again this year,
Friends islanded for the weekend.
To let him drive
To stop on the way
At the Narrows
For lunch, and let him pay.
The decision to walk the perimeter in the rain,
And glimpse the doe swimming over.
To let the breeze blow mist off the bay
And onto our twin sallow skins,
And let him use our names together.
The decision to let words breathe with wine—
Uncorked phrases aged more than a decade.
The decision to toast the setting sun
Falling beneath her watery azure curtain.
The decision to lie
Beneath a first-sighted Milky Way—
The lavender-blue satin ribbon imagined.
To break green mainland promises,
Like the glass carelessly placed
On the dark evening edge of warm
Concreted water bubbles.
To embrace Serenity,
But defy Courage and Wisdom.
The decision of a touch—
Handsome's devastation.
The decision to choose
To choose
To choose
A kiss
I cannot
Take back.
The decision
To come, again.

The Crossing

Like two Kandinski lines dancing
One raging orange (a pride of lions)
The other blue, perhaps Prussian
At the intersection of two stagnant planes—
Lies a mother's grown child scolded, enfolded
In the afternoon's deceitful prank.
More bewildered by punishment than Dante
Crossing through concentric circles into a cold Inferno,
Or Jordan waiting;
She is a worn wooden pick-up stick
                              gray as wind.
She confesses in guilty desperation
On the cathartic car ride with her
                    father
As they drive west, visors down, toward a lowing salmon
            sun—
That she's never felt so in-between
Like the vain attempt at crossing over from an early
      ghost.
What can she do?
A Crossing of the Self
In Prussian promise to the Other;
Her sins blamed all too mistakenly on
  A man.

Off-Shore

I miss him the way summer is missed—
that last skin glow,
a copper penny
born this year.
He is further off
than I think—

The shape of Parson's Island
as acres erode, more missing each season
changing this landscape;
this cliff of violets yawning
their blue defiance
at the waning Sunday sun.
Deer swim (though I did not know)
despite ivy poisoning the shore,
and run into the foliage
like a verdant secret.
His bay eyes left
to still me momentarily
in that green night.

The Ravine

In the dream he fell into the ravine
      a cleft in his chin
on his way to me
waiting like an orchid mountain
on the other side.
Twenty-five feet is far to fall;
His neck felt "funny"
His body, numb.
So I pull his arm across my shoulders
      where there once was water
in support of his dark figure.
My mother, in the card shop, offered
up Maryland General, unusually.

Over oatmeal, I told her. *Weird.*
His e-mail said he had a fever for two days.
Kayaking in wet clothes, she offered.
No. *The ravine.*

Thursday E-mail Check

Summer here in the east, a pewter puffer weed,
Is wished away
And then regretted
Like a false word to an older parent.
Each thought, a comma or momentary pause
A breath or beat
Origamied first on paper
And then a stroke of keys
Made careful as parchment
Finely worded in an eye of a needle.
With buttons as sealing wax
And a pony turned mouse,
The response is made in a space not understood;
A Faustian correspondence
More precious than spring
Water where expectation treads
A furious futile float.
And who thought of electronic mail as sustenance?
And who thought he would use the word,
beautiful?

Paradise

The curtains' gauzy yawn
Wakes me like a yellow ghost at the bottom of the bed
Yet I am startled by his figure—
Dark curls against the pale pillow linens,
His profile sleeping against the silhouette of dawn.
I long to extend my arm, a swan's neck,
Across the long expanse of this bed,
To trace his face with slender chalky finger
The way I long to touch Monet's
Oils leaning against the walls of the Walter's
And feel his brushstrokes as my own
And know the colors, the umber ringlets,
Sienna freckling the palette of the nose,
Pale Victorian rose of the lips;
But it's as if eyes watch warningly,
Preventing my finger's imprint;
The ducks call their morning sounds
In the hazel bay beyond this room
That mocks his closed eyes,
And still he lies with the rhythmic breath of slumber
Dreaming of white sails like windmills racing the wind.
But I know if I dare touch, I will disturb his mooring,
Oils breaking down under my acidic soothing.
I never remember the dream:
Last night he asked me to dance in these sheets,
Bodies in fluid motion under the full moon's liquid light,
But this morning, fear has come up with the sun,
And though I reach, I only venture to feel the electric fur
Of the space between finger and face
Before pulling back, my eyes doing lascivious feeling for me.

Friends

Went missing April Fool's
The cool white poster paper
Not smooth like his Irish skin or soft night curls;
Mystery thickens as this long day
That seems to breathe with heavy sighs
While fire burned his life away
Expelling charred clues like a phoenix
Onto the sidewalk
From the bowels of this Baltimore row house
Standing now bigger than itself
Like one of Poe's shadows:
A black leather shoe
Succumbed two-drawer file cabinet
Small empty safebox agape
Crushed box of chocolate top Berger cookies
A page of Achebe's *Things Fall Apart*—
The cinders of a child that never grew,
Trapped in a filmy haze, forever violet-blue.
His champagne Honda surfaces in Tennessee
Like a standard Loch Ness sighting;
Memphis medicine: a temporary fix,
Lost in that shadowed forest.
Virgil travels, continues the search,
As Baltimore vigils line pews and porch swings,
Trying to write the end of his book,
His memory gone missing, too.

The Daffodils

—*For Jimmy*

Pulling up curbside,
I notice
Even the daffodils
Are having a day—
Yellow heads fall heavy
Upon the early ground
Still in the fight for green.
Against the blue background
Of this failing day,
They are six-pointed stars
Worn on armbands in differentiation;
Their center reaching out
In some desperate hope
To catch and cup the dripping sun,
Just as my jaundiced faith
Lays heavy my head
Against this hard steering wheel.
I know I should tie tree ribbons for marines
Like my neighbors
Should be joy-stricken as the radio drones:
Red "terror alert" has been lowered to a yellow "elevated"
But I am blinded by the yellow-blue light of my own pain—
That selfish bending as if my whole body is genuflecting
In this little car:
It is the mourning of a childhood friend gone missing
The yellow face of fear caught in the rearview mirror,
Not mine, but his, in the westward running motion of escape.
Exiting the car, I stop and grab a clump of them by their
Thin green necks and pull up in a new surge of anger;
A ripping, a tearing, the surrender of earth's grasp.
Inside, I soften, place each of six in a clear glass jar.
They are his stars, shooting
Out of the water like flares
Heads newly uplifted
Signaling the way home.

Revolution

—*July 4, 2004*

The eruption of whistle and bang
Like blossoming gunshots
Call our attention upward from this pier;
We sit on the edge of a borrowed boat
Under champagne rain and violet stars—
Shapes that disappear as smoke
In celebration of freedom's reign.
This year I went sailing, turned thirty,
       added house keys to my ring.
He wants me to fly out west;
From Baltimore, Oregon is far for a first flight.
This is the year of my revolution.
I slow down in the thick collected waters
       of others' disapproval.
Or the waters of my own fear that have kept
Me grounded without white sail or wing.
But now he is my sail and he has opened my wings.
This is the year for my revolution.
In the smoky-orchid night sky,
Fire turns to birds of blue and red
       flying out from the center.
Sitting next to him, I do not think of specifics now,
But savor my wondrous smile
That comes only in bursts—
Astounding happiness sure to dissipate
Like these smoky remnants of Independence Day.
This is the year of my revolution.
And I am with him.
And I am not afraid.

The Relief of Spring

—For JCS

Shocking to the eye,
as the tulip
in its overnighting,
yellows to the bulbous sun;
He blooms in the deftness
of my light hand;
Fingers smooth-sanding
the plane of his back—
quenching an arid palm
reading the Braille of the skin.
He is the relief of spring;
His voice, childhood's pacifier
though at times an empty bottle.
Learning how to touch, tentative,
his tight-tendrilled curls
arbored to his mood.
Soon: the rains, that say
Water will drown the soil
Or water will fill the cup;
He is the lasting one
Tea-staining the tongue-
buds with astonishing beauty.
The tip of his own index finger
thickens like sailcloth
from the work that metamorphosizes
body into mythology;
the texture of change,
harder than March—
a year marking stone with an auger,
anger giving way to trust enwombed,
waiting to be born.

House-sitting

Perched at the top
Of the narrow back-stairs
Connecting the kitchen
And master bedroom
She calls to him:
Should we close their windows?
He joins her on this staircase
Though it is not theirs;
For a moment they are captured together—
A globe of fortune, a telling future,
The game of make-pretend called:
Domestic Circumstance.
She looks at him below her in the dim light
His curls blacker in the dusk,
Like the sharp edge of sobriety,
And leans against a goldenrod wall to let him pass,
Thinking how, certainly, she loves him.
Last night they dined against blooming wallpaper
And Victorian rose china, apple juice-filled crystal
Toasting a new year, though it was September,
Then climbed the stairs—
A barricade against the night.
Peeling off a silver necklace,
She dropped it to the dresser
Where she fingered the hound's tooth bottle
Of Channel No. 5 and some Parisian crème.
But now his body slides past her on the stairs,
And she is acutely aware of what he's going to do;
She breathes in, and is still as she listens,
The thrushing swoop and deadened thump,
A window closed.

Making Heat Waves

My mother wore silk nightgowns
In the Baltimore summers—
Fabric, she believed, would not stick
To her freckled skin.
Some were mint-green piped with baby's breath lace.
Her favorite, cornflower blue, like early morning
Ocean water once thought to ease pain.
Once.

Now I go to the shore for a swim
And am instantly aware of the stinging
Salt like nettles on my ankles,
Welts purple from the poison,
The itch like a thirst I cannot quench,
One water used to sate.
Once.

Jetty juts from the tip of the peninsula
Trying to wedge himself between water and shore—
A pushing away, sharp and slippery in the spray,
Seemingly insurmountable like
Hemmingway's white hills
And the color of my own remorse.
There, I look for relief, a delivered coolness.
But the silk sticks;
Sorrow's thirst unquenchable.
Expectations hang unmet
As seagulls sound overhead,
And I stand solitary
In disappointment's wake,
Disappointment
Like hot wind.

Escapism

My parents are in the den
Watching "Rockstar: INXS"
Father in the wingback, fading green to gray,
While mother crotchets a lavender blue scarf.
J. D. Fortune is debuting "Pretty Vegas"
As they watch on with abnormal normalcy
And I stand in the doorway
After coming in from the date
Attempting to normalize with them,
Though none of us escape
The undertones of malady,
Like a melody warning us
To get out of the water or
Pull back the shower's curtain.
But we cannot speak about it.
And I only manage an entertainment reference:
He sounds reincarnated.
And they acknowledge as best they can
Though I hear their quiet hurt in my head
While J. D. masks their air:
It ain't pretty when the pretty
Leaves you with no place to go.

Agape: The Millionth Bell

—For Beachy

The million bells are ringing out their purple glory;
Miniatures of their larger flower,
Pouring over the sides of the swinging basket
Like the molting feathers of a bluebird.
In their centers, ringers of yellow—
Heavenly eyes looking upon me this early morning,
Or perhaps mouths, agape in song, her song.
She is the millionth bell:
Her final ringing, a soprano chirp extended,
Softening at the edges like petals,
Before playing her last bell-in-cup game;
Or a tine's echo, rippling outward like clear water
Around a skimmed stone in a still lake,
Rings reaching outward like Jupiter's.
She was my friend in simplest form,
Asking for nothing but the quench of thirst, or
Millet for the belly, distending at the end
The way a child puffs out her chest in protest.
But she has not protested, giving in to this night,
Unable to drink from a dewy offering.
Her bell still ringing, becomes one of Jupiter's rings,
Aqua blue against the galaxy,
Her celestial song lingering in an orbit
My bird flies on her own.

On 30

—*January 4, 2004*

Today I saw black confetti
Falling from the day-gray sky—
A Hitchcock black-and-white
Viewed from my Tracker;
Thousands of birds as a moving cloud
Or silken ebony ribbon rippling
Down the velvet bodice of afternoon;
Or perhaps a swarm of bees
Toward the November-barren honeyed field
Where corn once thrived and grew,
Clamoring like playgrounded children.

I longed for half my life back;
Greenly planted in the field of fifteen,
Instead of gliding just over its reach
With extended wing, red-feathered.
Fifteen tasted like orange crush and poker,
First crush's sticky blushed lips,
Golden apples fresh from the tree.
Fifteen held buttercups under my chin.

But now the dandelions color my pallor,
Trying to outgrow themselves,
(Twice as high as the buttercups)
Extending their thin jade arms as if to say:
Pick me up; save me from my earthen self.
Wind blows through their yellow hair
And they bend as in the instant before
Birthday candles hush out their wish.
In the wind their flame turns to smoky ash,
Disappearing into the afternoon,
Like black confetti.

Bibliographical Note

Brooke Bognanni is a graduate of Friends School, Loyola College, and Loyola Graduate School, and holds BAs in Writing and Psychology, and a Master's Degree with a Writing concentration. Named *Who's Who Among America's Teachers*, she has taught at Loyola College and currently teaches at the Community College of Baltimore County. She splits her time living between Baltimore and the Eastern Shore of Maryland, has a fiancé, and two devoted parents.